IRISH UKULELE SONGBOOK

ISBN 978-1-4950-9902-1

Copyright © 2018 by HAL LEONARD LLC
International Copyright Secured   All Rights Reserved

Visit Hal Leonard Online at
www.halleonard.com

Contact Us:
Hal Leonard
7777 West Bluemound Road
Milwaukee, WI 53213
Email: info@halleonard.com

In Europe contact:
Hal Leonard Europe Limited
42 Wigmore Street
Marylebone, London, W1U 2RN
Email: info@halleonardeurope.com

In Australia contact:
Hal Leonard Australia Pty. Ltd.
4 Lentara Court
Cheltenham, Victoria, 3192 Australia
Email: info@halleonard.com.au

Believe Me, If All Those
Endearing Young Charms

Words and Music by Thomas Moore

First note

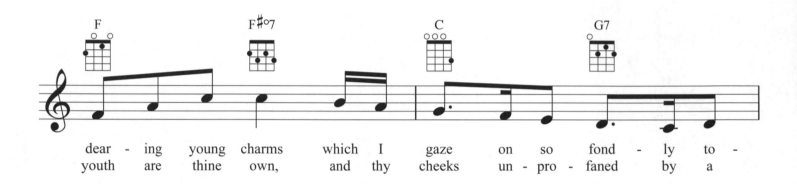

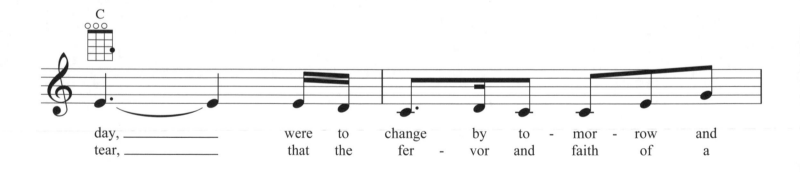

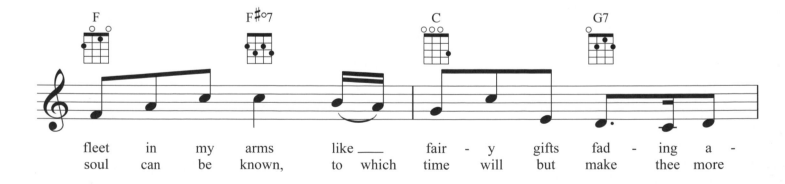

way, _____ thou would'st still be a - dored as this
dear! _____ No, the heart that has tru - ly loved

mo - ment thou art let thy love - li - ness fade as it
nev - er for - gets, but as tru - ly loves on to the

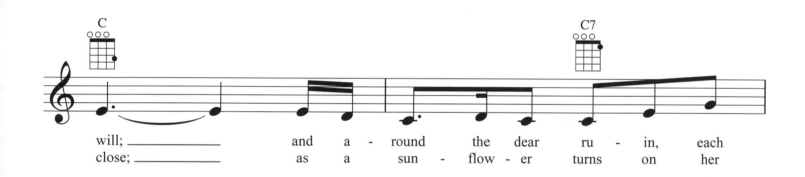

will; _____ and a - round the dear ru - in, each
close; _____ as a sun - flow - er turns on her

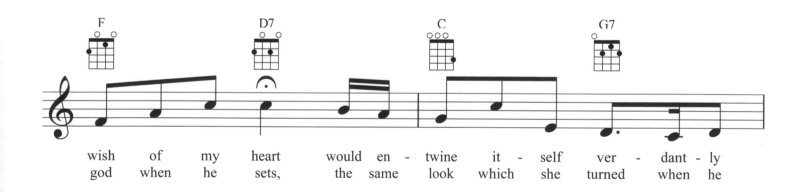

wish of my heart, would en - twine it - self ver - dant - ly
god when he sets, would the same look which she turned when he

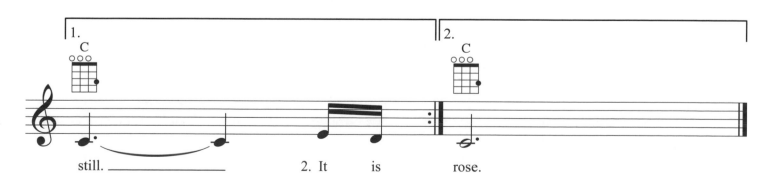

still. _____ 2. It is rose.

Black Velvet Band

Traditional Irish Folk Song

Broad - way, _____ not in - tend - ing to
morn - ing, _____ both of us

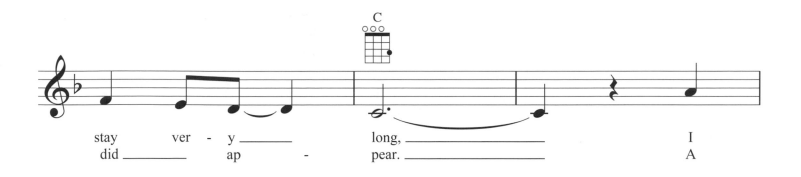

C

stay ver - y _____ long, _____ I
did _____ ap - pear. _____ A

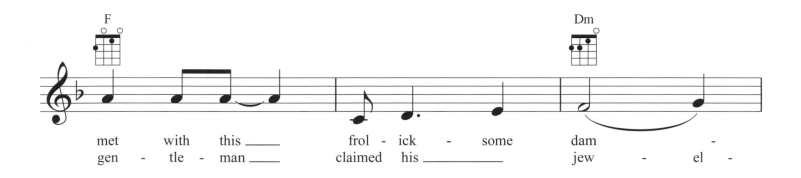

F   Dm

met with this _____ frol - ick - some dam -
gen - tle - man _____ claimed his _____ jew - el -

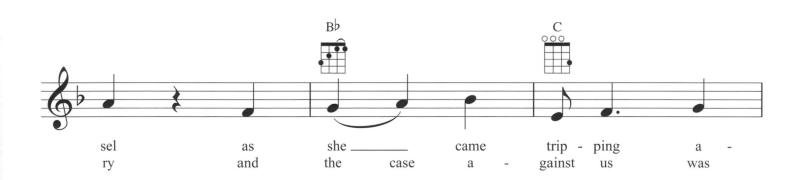

Bb   C

sel   as she _____ came trip - ping a -
ry   and the case a - gainst us was

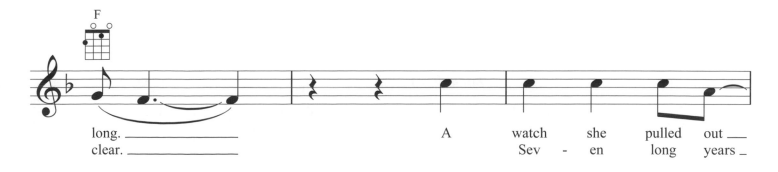

F

long. _____ A watch she pulled out _____
clear. _____ Sev - en long years _

_____ of her _____ pock - et _____ and

_____ trans - por - ta - tion _____ right

slipped it right _____ in - to me _____ hand. _____ On the

on down to _____ Van Die - men's _ Land; _____ far a -

ver - y first day that I _____ met _____ her, bad

way from my friends and com - pan - ions to

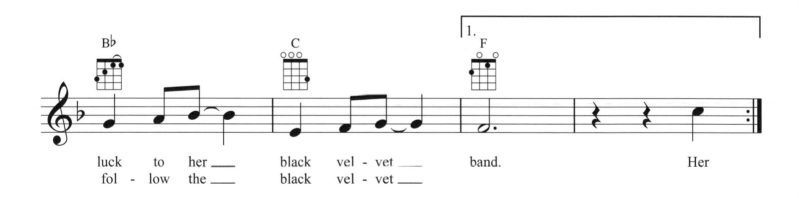

1.

luck to her _____ black vel - vet _____ band. Her

fol - low the _____ black vel - vet _____

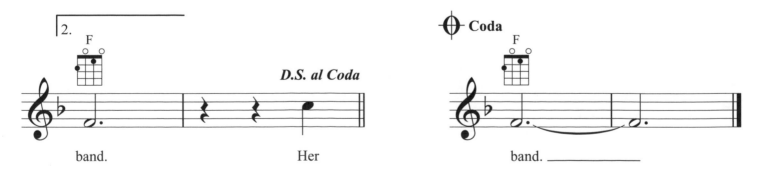

2.

D.S. al Coda

band. Her

Coda

band. _____

The Galway Piper

Irish Folksong

Carrickfergus

Traditional Irish Folk Song

grant. But the sea is wide _____
drink. I'm _____ drunk to - day, _____

_____ and I can't swim o - ver, _____ nor have _____
_____ but then I'm sel - dom so - ber, _____ a hand - some

I _____ the _____ wings to fly. _____
rov - er _____ from _____ town to town. _____

_____ If I could find me _____ a _____ hand - some
_____ Ah, but I'm sick now, _____ my _____ days are

boats - man _____ to fer - ry me o - ver _____ to my love and
o - ver. _____ Come, all ye young lads, _____ and _ lay me

1.   2.

die.   2. Now in Kil - down. _____

The Croppy Boy

Eighteenth Century Irish Folk Song

First note

Moderately **Verse**

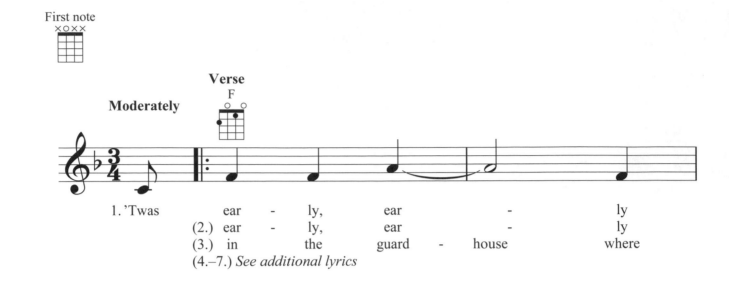

1. 'Twas ear - ly, ear - ly
(2.) ear - ly, ear - ly
(3.) in the guard - house where
(4.–7.) *See additional lyrics*

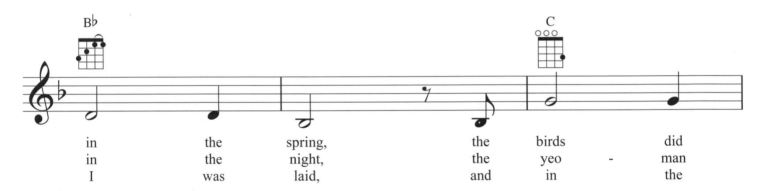

in the spring, the birds did
in the night, the yeo - man
I was laid, and in the

whis - tle and sweet - ly sing, _____
cav - al - ry gave me a fright.
par - lor where I was tried. _____

chang - ing their notes from tree to tree, _____
The yeo - man cav - al - ry was my down -
My sen - tence passed and my cour - age low, _____

Additional Lyrics

4. As I was passing my father's door, my brother William stood at the door.
   My aged father stood there also, my tender mother her hair she tore.

5. As I was going up Wexford Hill, who could blame me to cry my fill?
   I looked behind and I looked before, my aged mother I shall see no more.

6. As I was mounted on the scaffold high, my aged father was standing by.
   My aged father did me deny, and the name he gave me was the croppy boy.

7. 'Twas in the Dungannon this young man died, and in Dungannon his body lies.
   And you good people that do pass by, oh, shed a tear for the croppy boy.

Danny Boy

Words by Frederick Edward Weatherly
Traditional Irish Folk Melody

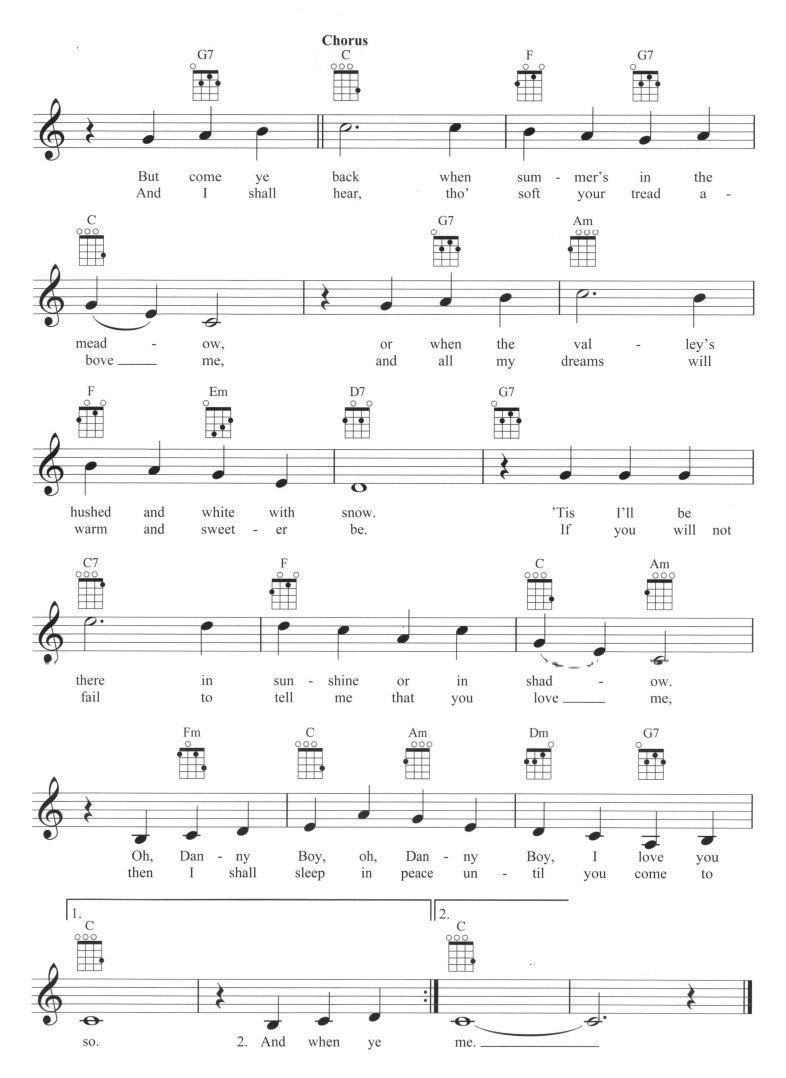

Down by the Salley Gardens

Traditional Irish Folk Song

First note

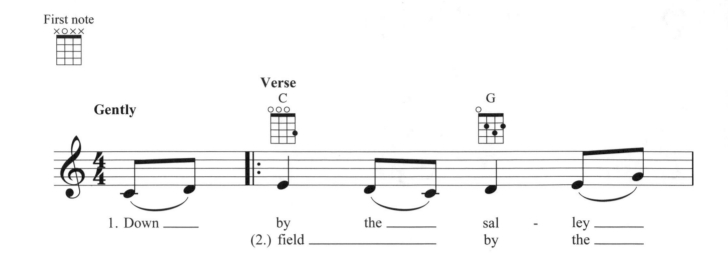

Gently   Verse

1. Down ____ by the ____ sal - ley ____
(2.) field _____ by the ____

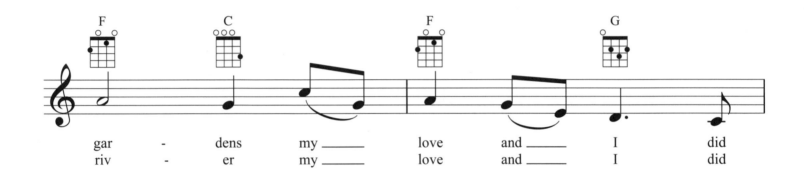

gar - dens my ____ love and ____ I did
riv - er my ____ love and ____ I did

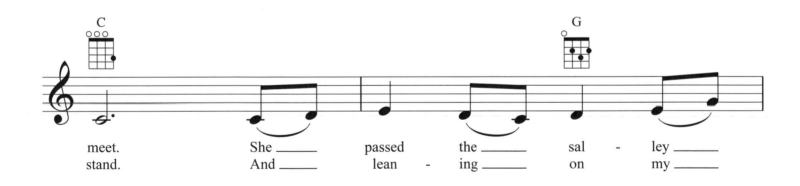

meet. She ____ passed the ____ sal - ley ____
stand. And ____ lean - ing ____ on my ____

gar - dens with ____ lit - tle ____ snow - white
shoul - der she ____ laid her ____ snow - white

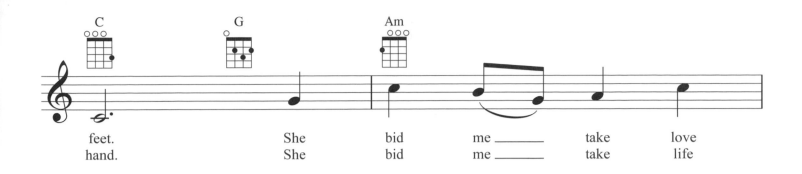

feet.   She   bid   me _____ take   love

hand.   She   bid   me _____ take   life

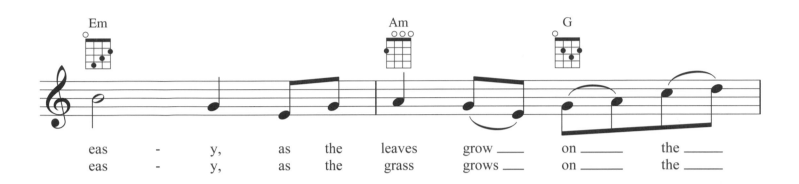

eas - y,   as   the   leaves   grow _____ on _____ the _____

eas - y,   as   the   grass   grows _____ on _____ the _____

tree.   But _____ I,   be - ing   young   and _____

weirs.   But _____ I   was _____ young   and _____

fool - ish,   with _____ her   did _____ not   a -

fool - ish,   and _____ now   am _____ full   of

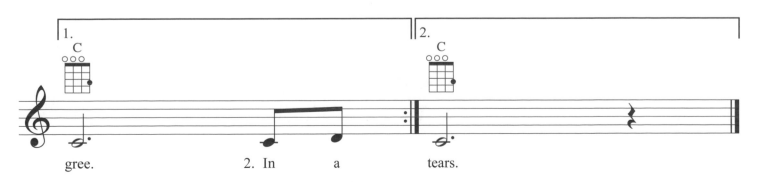

gree.   2. In   a   tears.

The Fields of Athenry

Words and Music by Pete St. John

morn. Now a pris - on ship lies wait - ing in the bay." _____
down, now you must raise our child with dig - ni - ty." _____
Bay, it's so lone - ly 'round the fields of Ath - en - ry. _____

Chorus

_____ Low, lie the fields _____ of Ath - en -

ry, where once we watched the small free birds fly. _____

_____ Our _ love was on the wing, we had dreams and songs _ to

sing. It's so lone - ly 'round the fields of Ath - en -

ry. _____   1., 2.   3.

2. By a _____
3. By a

Finnegan's Wake

Traditional Irish Folk Song

First note

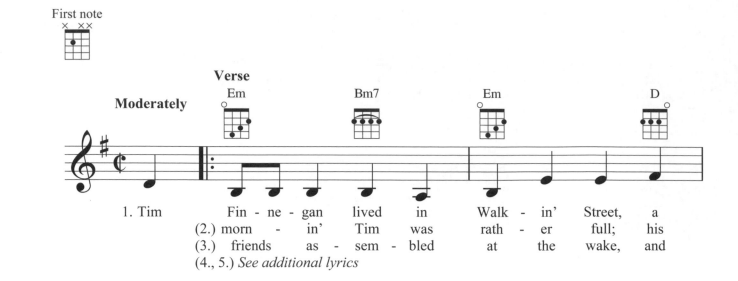

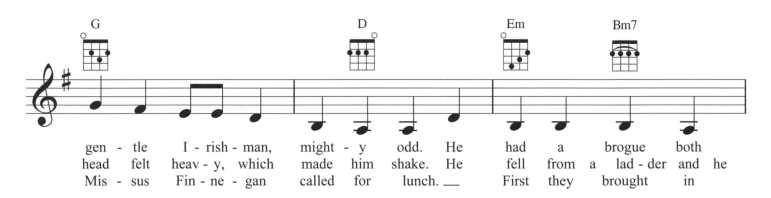

1. Tim Fin - ne - gan lived in Walk - in' Street, a
(2.) morn - in' Tim was rath - er full; his
(3.) friends as - sem - bled at the wake, and
(4., 5.) *See additional lyrics*

gen - tle I - rish - man, might - y odd. He had a brogue both
head felt heav - y, which made him shake. He fell from a lad - der and he
Mis - sus Fin - ne - gan called for lunch. ___ First they brought in

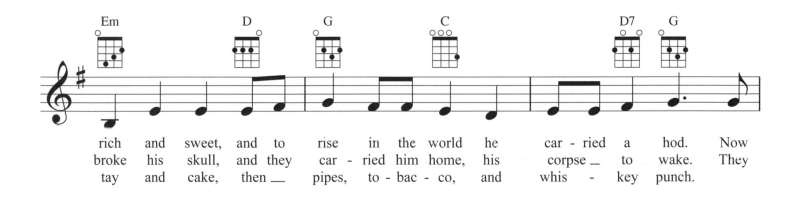

rich and sweet, and to rise in the world he car - ried a hod. Now
broke his skull, and they car - ried him home, his corpse ___ to wake. They
tay and cake, then ___ pipes, to - bac - co, and whis - key punch.

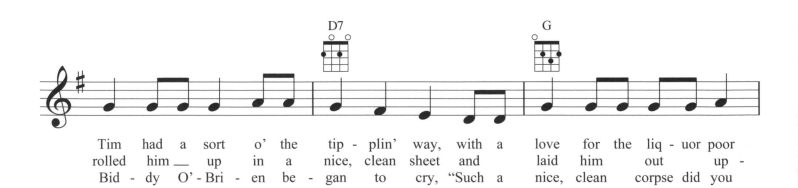

Tim had a sort o' the tip - plin' way, with a love for the liq - uor poor
rolled him ___ up in a nice, clean sheet and laid him out up -
Bid - dy O' - Bri - en be - gan to cry, "Such a nice, clean corpse did you

19

Additional Lyrics

4. Then Maggie O'Connor took up the job,
   "Oh, Biddy," says she, "you're wrong, I'm sure."
   Biddy, she gave her a belt in the gob
   And left her sprawlin' on the floor.
   And then the war did soon engage,
   'Twas woman to woman and man to man.
   Shillelaigh law was all the rage,
   And a row and ruction soon began.

5. Then Mickey Maloney ducked his head
   When a noggin of whiskey flew at him.
   It missed, and falling on the bed,
   The liquor scattered over Tim!
   The corpse revives; see how he rises!
   Timothy, rising from the bed,
   Said, "Whirl your whiskey around like blazes,
   Thanum an Dhul! Do you think I'm dead?"

The Foggy Dew

Traditional Irish Folk Song

First note

Verse
Moderately slow

1. O - ver the hills I ____ went one
2. O - ver the hills I ____ went one

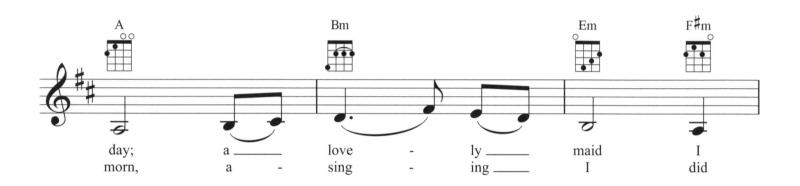

day; a ____ love - ly ____ maid I
morn, a - sing - ing ____ I did

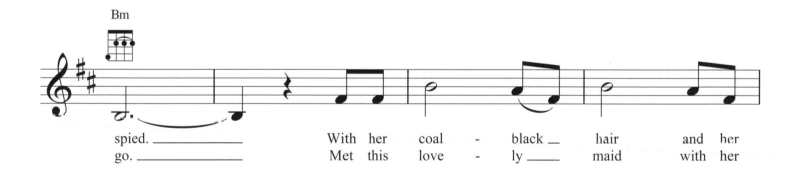

spied. _____ With her coal - black ____ hair and her
go. _____ Met this love - ly ____ maid with her

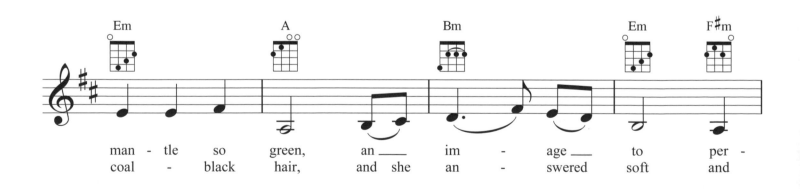

man - tle so green, an ____ im - age ____ to per -
coal - black hair, and she an - swered soft and

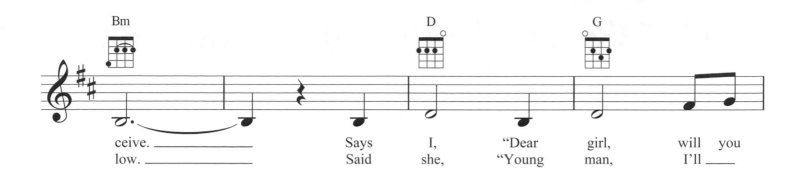

ceive. _____ Says I, "Dear girl, will you
low. _____ Said she, "Young man, I'll ____

be my ___ bride?" And she lift - ed her eyes of ____
be your ___ bride, if I know ___ her that eyes you'll be ____

blue. _____ She smiled and ___ said, "Young man,
true." _____ Oh, in my ___ arms, all ____

I'm to wed; I'm to meet him in the fog - gy
of her charms were ___ cast - ed in the fog - gy

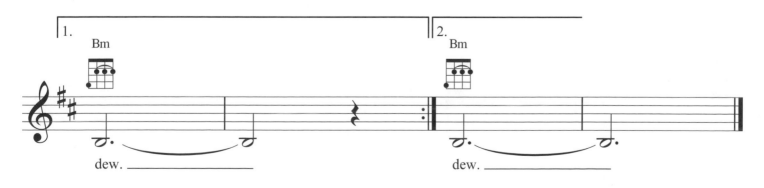

1.
dew. _____

2.
dew. _____

I'll Take You Home Again, Kathleen

Words and Music by Thomas Westendorf

Chorus

watched them fade a - way and die, your
side your moth - er's hum - ble cot your and

voice is sad when - e'er you speak and
bright - est rays of sun - shine gleam, there

tears be - dim your lov - ing eyes. ⎫
all your grief will be for - got. ⎭ Oh,

I will take you back, Kath - leen, to where your heart will feel no

pain. And when the fields are fresh and green, I'll ___

take you to your home, Kath - leen. ___ 2. To leen.

I'll Tell Me Ma

Traditional Irish Folk Song

First note

Verse
Moderately fast

1. I'll tell me ma, when I go home, the
(2.) Al - bert Moon - ey says he loves her;
(3.) wind and the rain and the hail blow high and the

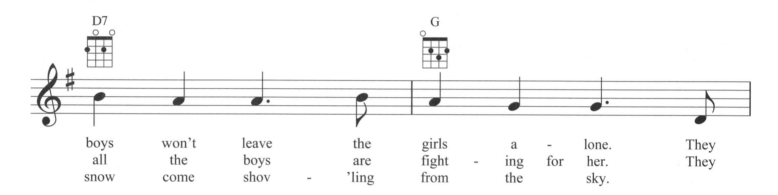

boys won't leave the girls a - lone. They
all the boys are fight - ing for her. They
snow come shov - 'ling from the sky.

pull my hair, they stole my comb, and
rap at the door and ring the bell, say - ing,
She's as nice as ap - ple pie, and she'll

that's al - right till I go home.
"Oh, my true love, are you well?"
get her own lad by and by.

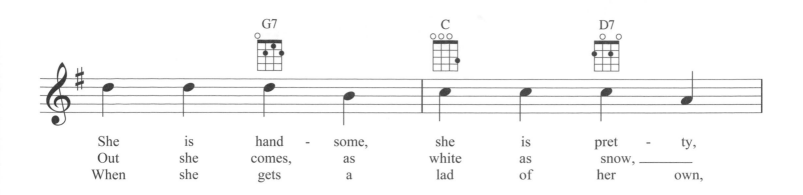

She is hand - some, she is pret - ty,
Out she comes, as white is as snow, _____
When she gets a lad of her own,

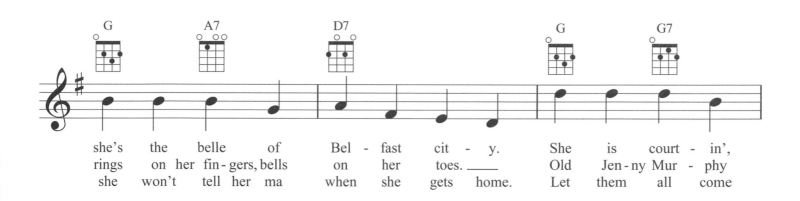

she's the belle of Bel - fast cit - y. She is court - in',
rings on her fin-gers, bells on her toes. _____ Old Jen-ny Mur - phy
she won't tell her ma when she gets home. Let them all come

one, two, three. Please, won't you tell me
says she'll die if she does - n't get the fel - low
as they will, but it's Al - bert Moon - ey

1., 2.
who is she? 2. Now,
with the rov - ing eye. 3. Let the

3.
she loves still.

The Irish Rover

Traditional Irish Folk Song

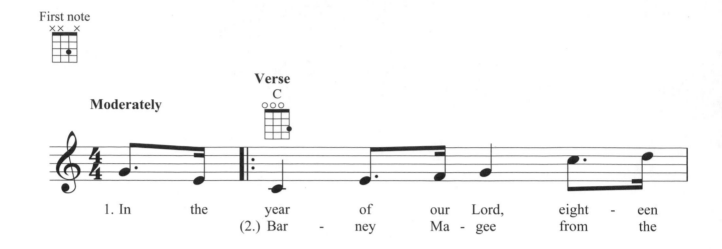

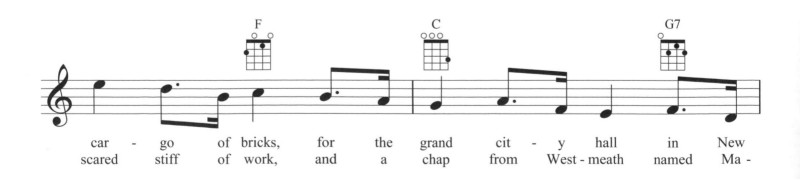

York. We'd an el - e - gant craft, it was
lone. There was Slug - ger O' - Toole, who was

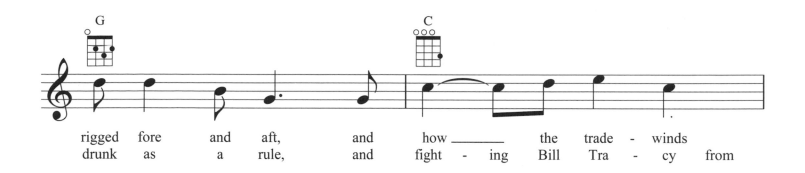

rigged fore and aft, and how _____ the trade - winds
drunk as a rule, and fight - ing Bill Tra - cy from

drove _____ her. She had twen - ty - three masts and she
Do - ver. And your man Mick Mc - Cann, from she the

stool sev - 'ral blasts, and they called her the I - rish
banks of the Bann, was the skip - per on the I - rish

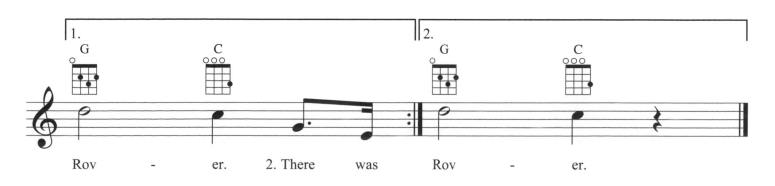

Rov - er. 2. There was Rov - er.

The Irish Washerwoman

Irish Folk Song

Red Is the Rose

Irish Folk Song

First note

bon - ny   I - rish   lass, _____
wood - lands   that   we   stayed, _____
dar - ling   girl   is   gone. _____
my _____   sis - ter   pains, _____

come   o - ver   the   hills   to   your
the   moon   and   the   stars   they   were
She's   gone   and   met   with   an -
not   for   the   grief   of   my _____

dar   -   ling. _____   You
shin   -   ing. _____   The   moon
oth   -   er. _____   I'm   full
moth   -   er. _____   It's   all

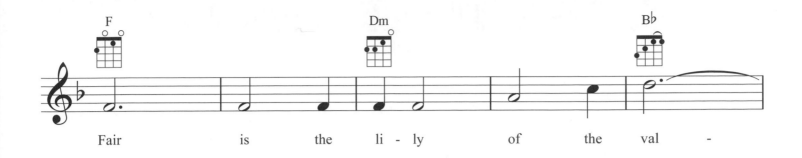

Fair   is   the   li - ly   of   the   val -

-    ley. _____   Clear   is   the

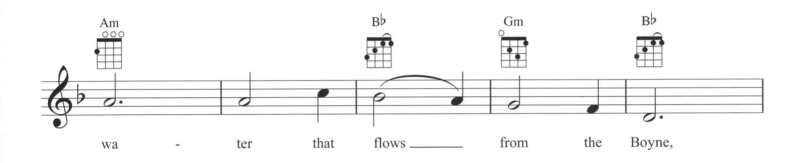

wa -   ter   that   flows _____ from   the   Boyne,

but _____ my   love   is   fair -   er   than

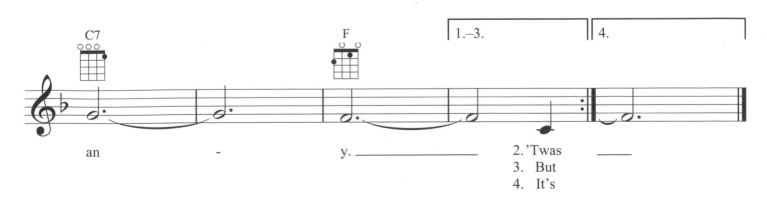

an -   y. _____   2. 'Twas _____
                                           3. But
                                         4. It's

Johnny, I Hardly Knew You

Traditional Irish Folk Song

First note

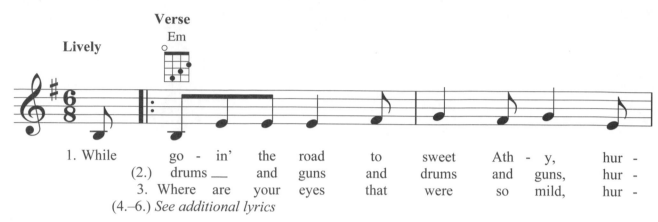

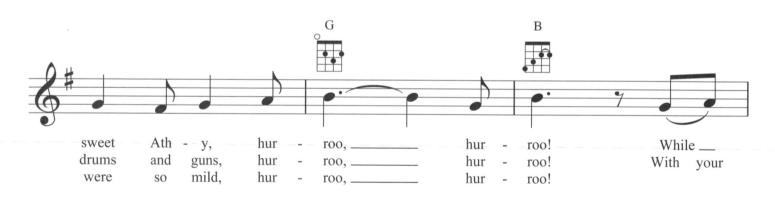

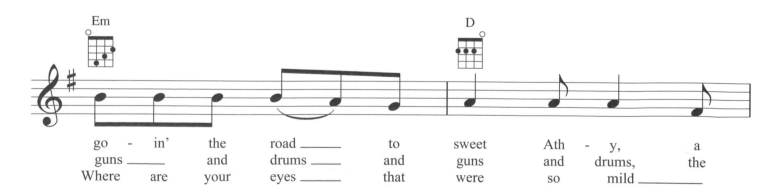

stick   in   me   hand   and   a   drop   in   me   eye, _____   a
en - e - my   near - ly   slew _____   me.   Oh, _____   my
when _____ my   heart _____ you   so _____   be - guiled? ___   Why

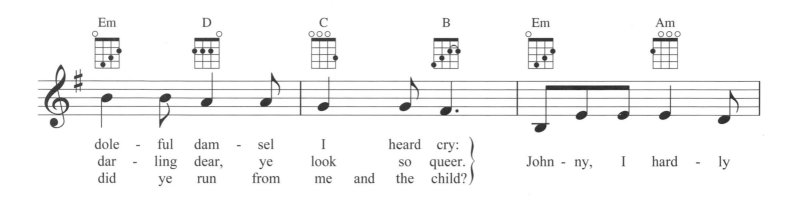

dole - ful   dam - sel   I   heard   cry: John - ny,   I   hard - ly
dar - ling   dear,   ye   look   so   queer.
did   ye   run   from   me   and   the   child?

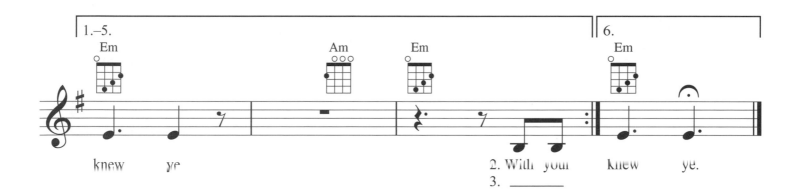

knew   ye   2. With your   knew   ye.
3. _____

Additional Lyrics

4. Where are your legs that used to run, hurroo, hurroo!
Where are your legs that used to run, hurroo, hurroo!
Where are your legs that used to run
When you went for to carry a gun?
Indeed, your dancing days are done.
Johnny, I hardly knew ye.

5. I'm happy for to see you home, hurroo, hurroo!
I'm happy for to see you home, hurroo, hurroo!
I'm happy for to see you home
All from the island of Sulloon,
So low in flesh, so high in bone.
Johnny, I hardly knew ye.

6. Ye haven't an arm, ye haven't a leg, hurroo, hurroo!
Ye haven't an arm, ye haven't a leg, hurroo, hurroo!
Ye haven't an arm, ye haven't a leg,
Ye're an armless, boneless, chickenless egg.
Ye'll have to put with a bowl out to beg.
Johnny, I hardly knew ye.

MacNamara's Band

Words by John J. Stamford
Music by Shamus O'Connor

1. Oh! Me name is Mac - Na - ma - ra, I'm the
2. Now we are re - hears - in' for a

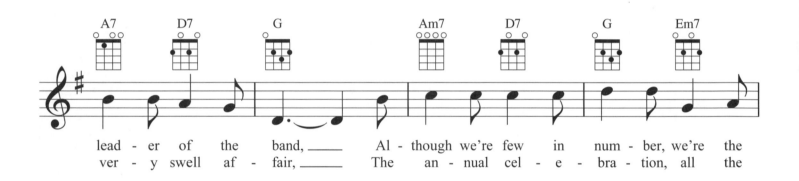

lead - er of the band, _____ Al - though we're few in num - ber, we're the
ver - y swell af - fair, _____ The an - nual cel - e - bra - tion, all the

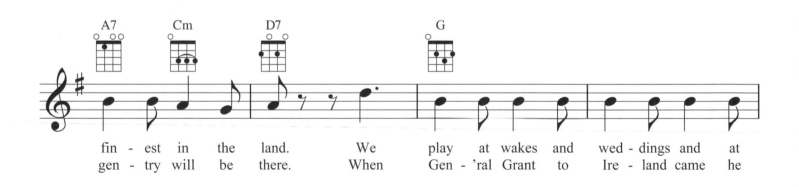

fin - est in the land. We play at wakes and wed - dings and at
gen - try will be there. When Gen - 'ral Grant to Ire - land came he

ev - 'ry fan - cy ball, _____ And when we play at fun - er - als we
took me by the hand, _____ Says he, "I nev - er saw the likes of

Minstrel Boy

Traditional

First note

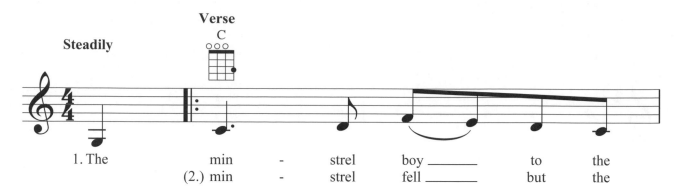

Steadily   **Verse**

1. The min - strel boy _____ to the
(2.) min - strel boy fell _____ but the

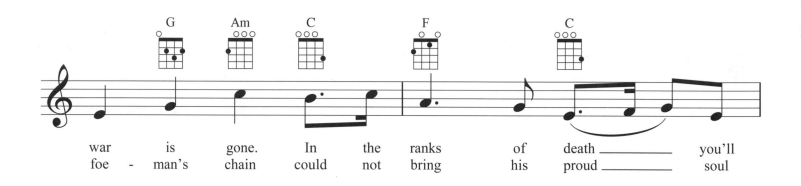

war is gone. In the ranks of death _____ you'll
foe - man's chain could not bring his proud _____ soul

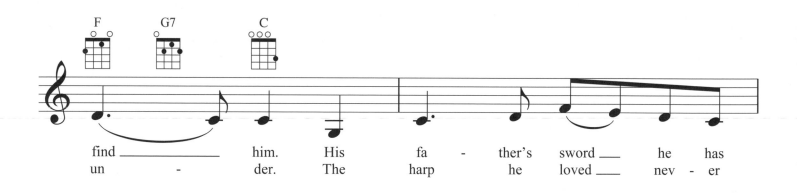

find _____ him. His fa - ther's sword ___ he has
un - der. The harp he loved ___ nev - er

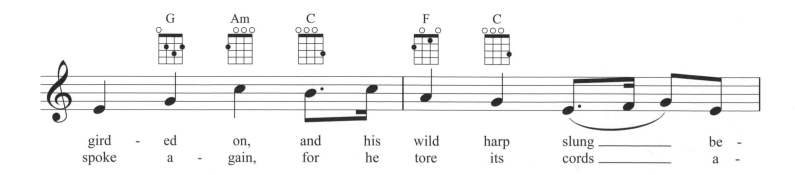

gird - ed on, and his wild harp slung _____ be -
spoke a - gain, for he tore its cords _____ a -

Molly Malone
(Cockles & Mussels)
Irish Folk Song

First note

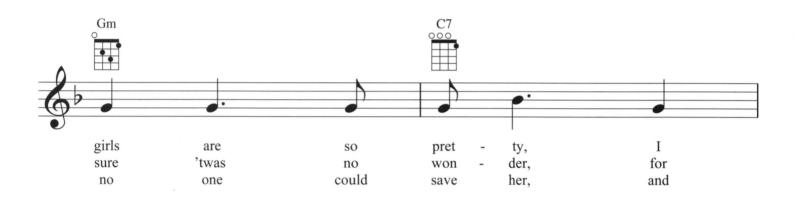

1. In Dub - lin's fair cit - y, where
(2.) was a fish - mon - ger, but
(3.) died of a fe - ver, and

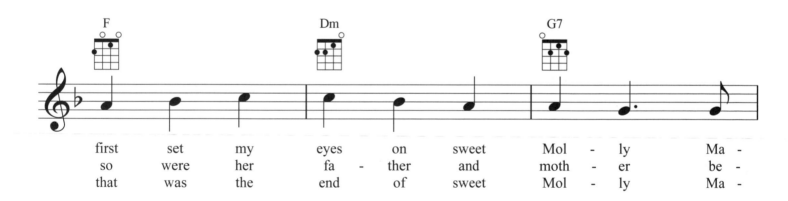

girls are so pret - ty, I
sure 'twas no won - der, for
no one could save her, and

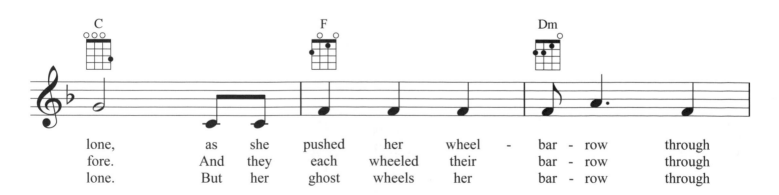

first set my eyes on sweet Mol - ly Ma -
so were her fa - ther and moth - er be -
that was the end of sweet Mol - ly Ma -

lone, as she pushed her wheel - bar - row through
fore. And they each wheeled their bar - row through
lone. But her ghost wheels her bar - row through

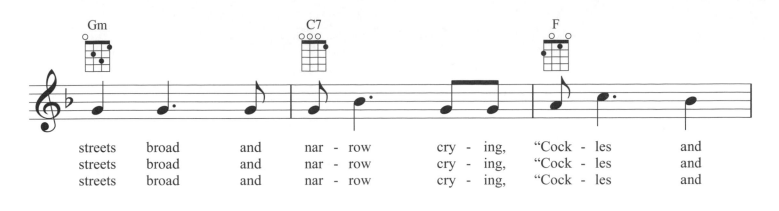

streets   broad   and   nar - row   cry - ing,   "Cock - les   and
streets   broad   and   nar - row   cry - ing,   "Cock - les   and
streets   broad   and   nar - row   cry - ing,   "Cock - les   and

mus - sels,   a - live,   a - live,   oh!   A -
mus - sels,   a - live,   a - live,   oh!
mus - sels,   a - live,   a - live,   oh!

Chorus

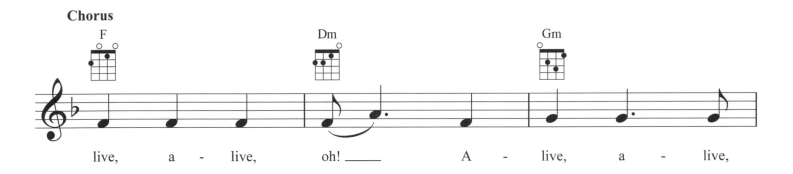

live,   a - live,   oh! ___   A - live,   a - live,

oh!" ___   Cry - ing,   "Cock - les   and   mus - sels,   a -

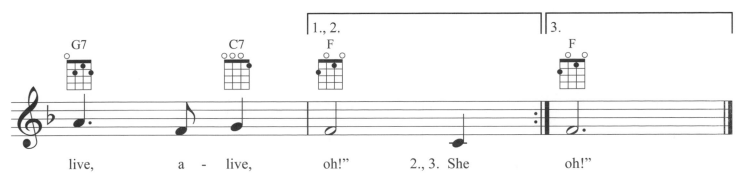

live,   a - live,   oh!"   2., 3. She   oh!"

My Wild Irish Rose

Words and Music by Chauncey Olcott

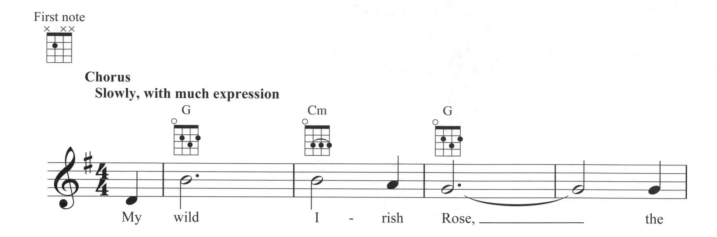

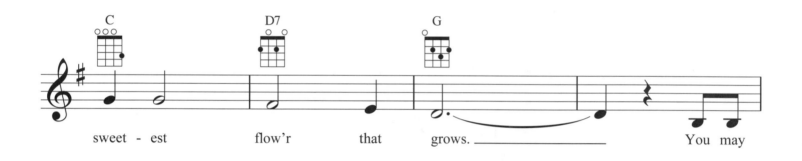

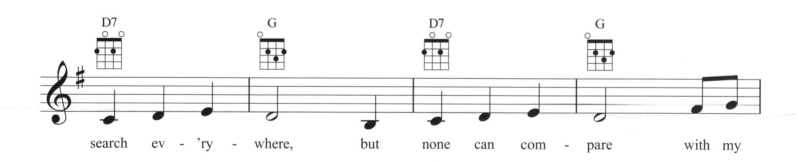

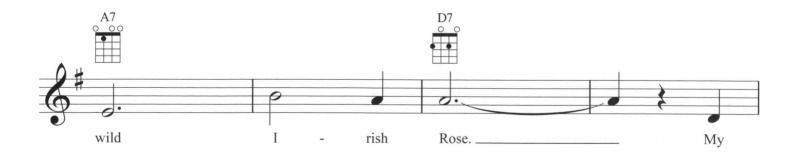

wild   I - rish   Rose, _____

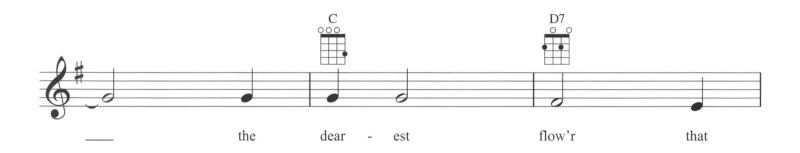

_____   the   dear - est   flow'r   that

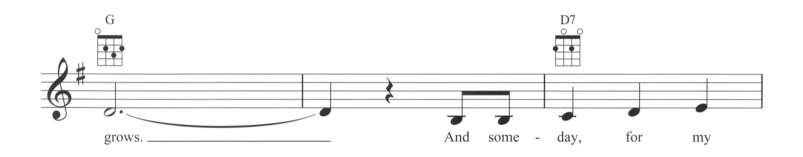

grows. _____   And   some - day,   for   my

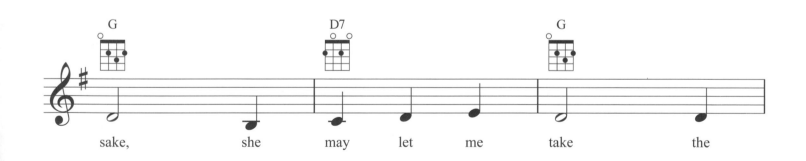

sake,   she   may   let   me   take   the

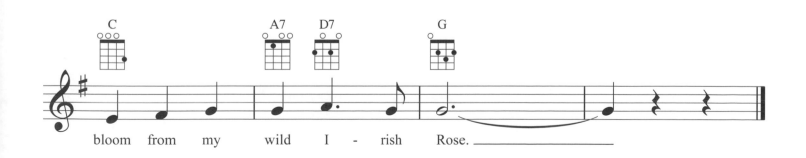

bloom from my wild   I - rish Rose. _____

The Parting Glass

Irish Folk Song

First note

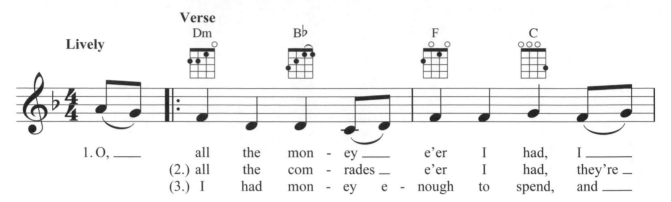

1. O, _____ all the mon - ey _____ e'er I had, I _____
(2.) all the com - rades _____ e'er I had, they're _____
(3.) I had mon - ey e - nough to spend, and _____

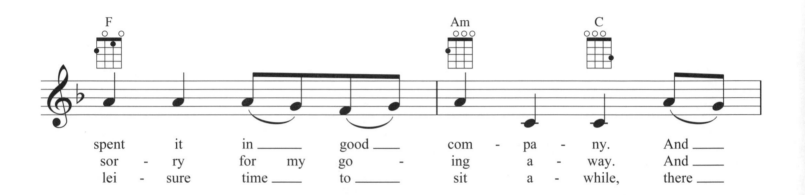

spent it in _____ good _____ com - pa - ny. And _____
sor - ry for my go - ing a - way. And _____
lei - sure time _____ to _____ sit a - while, there _____

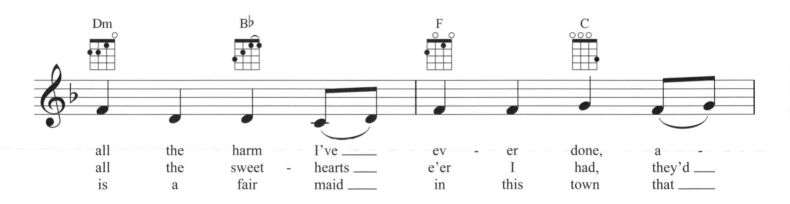

all the harm I've _____ ev - er done, a -
all the sweet - hearts _____ e'er I had, they'd _____
is a fair maid _____ in this town that _____

las, it was _____ to _____ none but me. And
wish me one _____ more _____ day to stay. But
sore - ly has _____ my _____ heart be - guiled. Her

The Rose of Tralee

Words by C. Mordaunt Spencer
Music by Charles W. Glover

First note

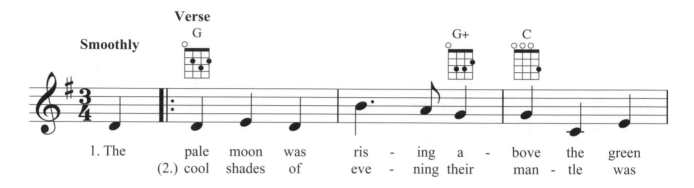

1. The pale moon was ris - ing a - bove the green
(2.) cool shades of eve - ning their man - tle was

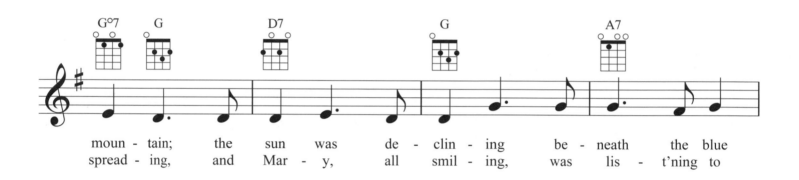

moun - tain; the sun was de - clin - ing be - neath the blue
spread - ing, and Mar - y, all smil - ing, was lis - t'ning to

sea when I strayed with my love to the pure crys - tal
me. The moon through the val - ley her pure pale rays was

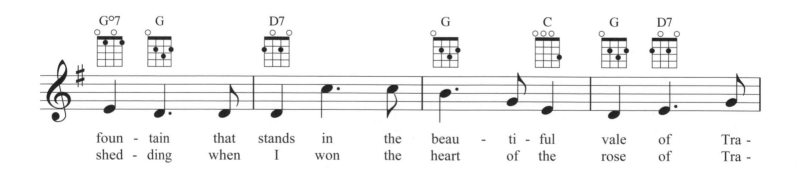

foun - tain that stands in the beau - ti - ful vale of Tra -
shed - ding when I won the heart of the rose of Tra -

Chorus

lee.   She was } love - ly   and   fair   as   the
lee.   Though __ }

rose   of ____   the ____   sum - mer,   yet   'twas   not   her

beau - ty   a - lone   that   won   me.   Oh,   no!   'Twas   the

truth   in   her   eye   ev - er   dawn - ing   that   made   me   love

Mar - y,   the   rose   of   Tra - lee.

2. The

Too-Ra-Loo-Ra-Loo-Ral
(That's an Irish Lullaby)

Words and Music by James R. Shannon

1. O - ver in Kil - lar - ney, _____
2. Oft, in dreams I wan - der _____

man - y years a - go, me
to that cot a - gain, I

moth - er sang a song to me in
feel her arms a hug - gin' me as

tones so sweet and low. Just a sim - ple
when she held me then. And I hear her

lit - tle dit - ty, in her good old
voice a hum - min' to me as in

Too - ra - loo - ra - loo - ral, _____

_____ too - ra - loo - ra - li, _____

_____ too - ra - loo - ra - loo - ral,

that's an I - rish lull - a -

by. _____ loo - ral, that's an

I - rish lull - a - by. _____

Seven Drunken Nights

Traditional Irish Folk Song

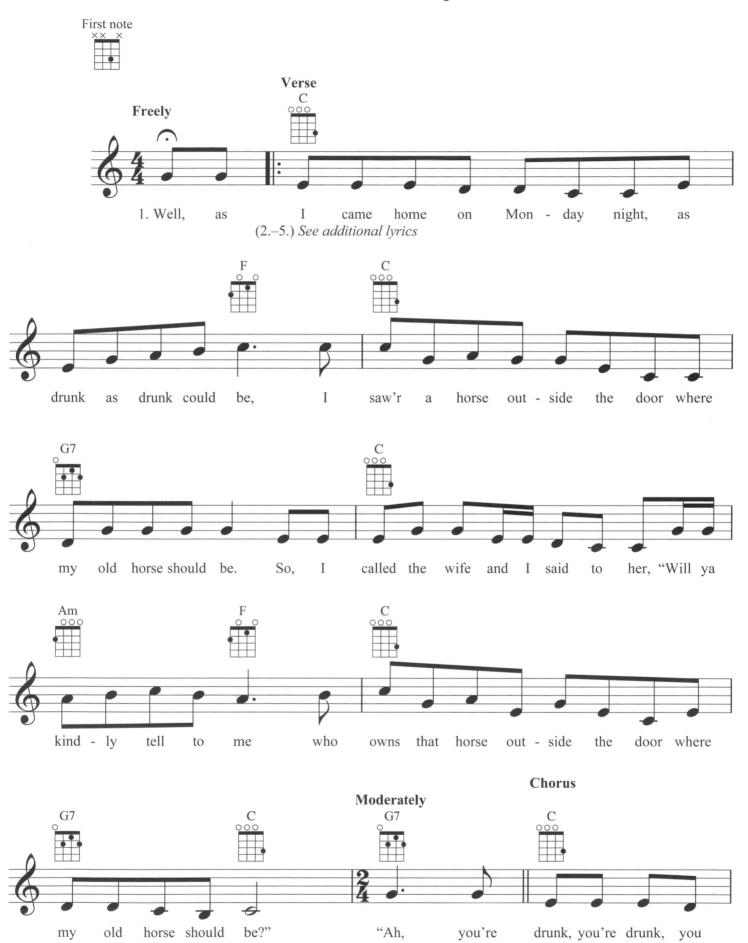

sil - ly old fool, un - til you can - not see. And

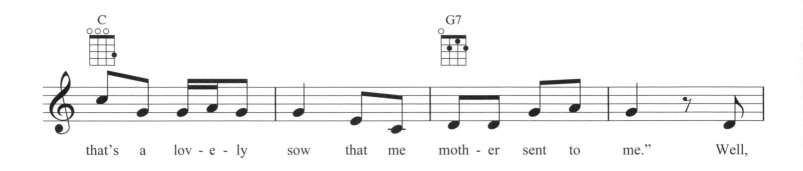

that's a lov - e - ly sow that me moth - er sent to me." Well,

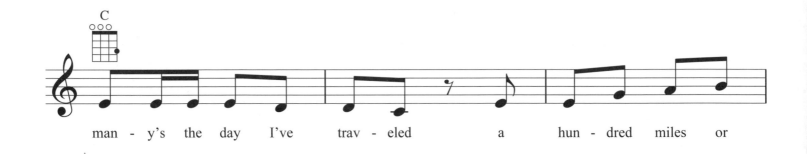

man - y's the day I've trav - eled a hun - dred miles or

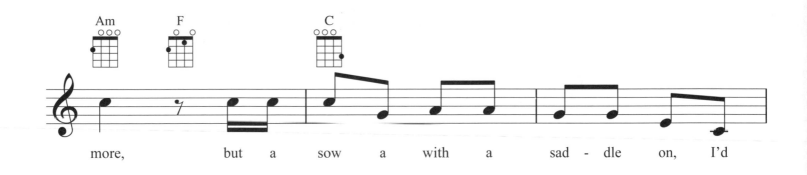

more, but a sow a with a sad - dle on, I'd

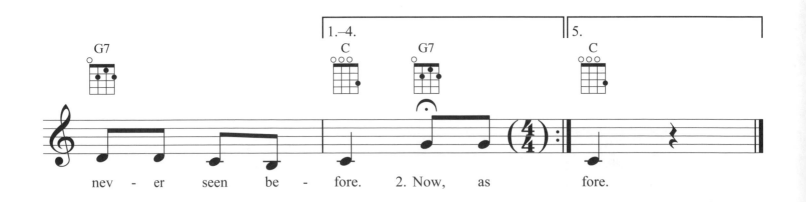

nev - er seen be - fore. 2. Now, as fore.

Additional Lyrics

2. Now, as I came home on Tuesday night,
   As drunk as drunk could be,
   I saw'r a coat behind the door
   Where my old coat should be.
   So I called the wife and I said to her,
   "Will ya kindly tell to me,
   Who owns that coat behind the door
   Where my old coat should be?"

Chorus: "Ah, you're drunk, you're drunk, you silly old fool, till you cannot see.
   That's a lovely blanket that me mother sent to me."
   Well, many's the day I traveled a hundred miles or more,
   But buttons on a blanket sure I never seen before.

3. And as I went home on Wednesday night,
   As drunk as drunk could be,
   I saw'r a pipe upon the chair
   Where my old pipe should be.
   I calls the wife and I says to her,
   "Will ya kindly tell to me,
   Who owns that pipe upon the chair
   Where my old pipe should be?"

Chorus: "Ah, you're drunk, you're drunk, you silly old fool, still you cannot see.
   And that's a lovely tin whistle that me mother sent to me."
   Well, and many's the day I've traveled a hundred miles or more,
   But tobacco in a tin whistle sure I never seen before.

4. And as I went home on Thursday night,
   As drunk as drunk could be,
   I saw'r two boots beneath the bed
   Where my two boots should be.
   I called the wife and I said to her,
   "Will ya kindly tell to me,
   Who owns those boots beneath the bed
   Where my old boots should be?"

Chorus: "Ah, you're drunk, you're drunk, you silly old fool, until you cannot see.
   And that's me lovely geranium pots me mother sent to me."
   Well, it's many's the day I've traveled a hundred miles or more,
   But laces on a geranium pot I never seen before.

5. And as I went home on Friday night,
   As drunk as drunk could be,
   I saw'r a head upon the bed
   Where my old head should be.
   So, I called the wife and I said to her,
   "Will ya kindly tell to me,
   Who owns that head upon the bed
   Where my old head should be?"

Chorus: "Ah, you're drunk, you're drunk, you silly old fool, and still you cannot see.
   That's a baby boy that me mother sent to me."
   Hey, it's many's the day I've traveled a hundred miles or more,
   But a baby boy with whiskers on I never seen before.

Spancil Hill

Traditional Irish Folk Song

First note

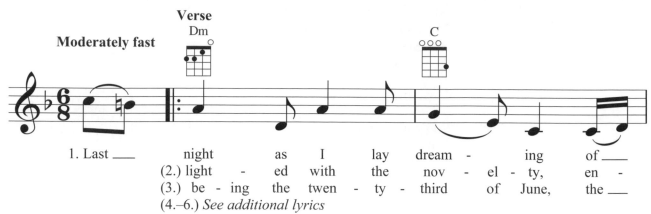

Moderately fast   **Verse**

1. Last ___ night as I lay dream - ing of ___
(2.) light - ed with the nov - el - ty, en -
(3.) be - ing the twen - ty - third of June, the ___
(4.–6.) *See additional lyrics*

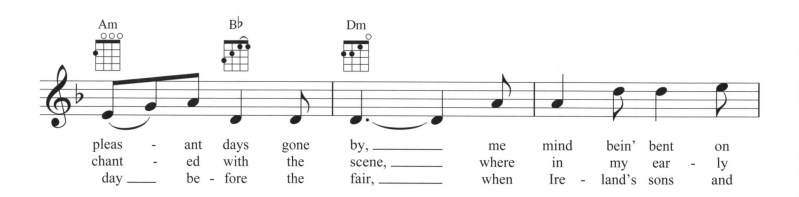

pleas - ant days gone by, _____ me mind bein' bent on
chant - ed with the scene, _____ where in my ear - ly
day ___ be - fore the fair, _____ when Ire - land's sons and

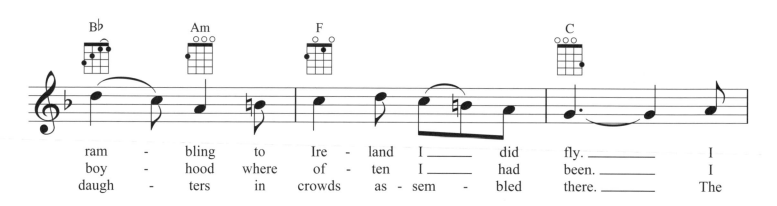

ram - bling to Ire - land I ___ did fly. _____ I
boy - hood where of - ten I ___ had been. _____ I
daugh - ters in crowds as - sem - bled there. _____ The

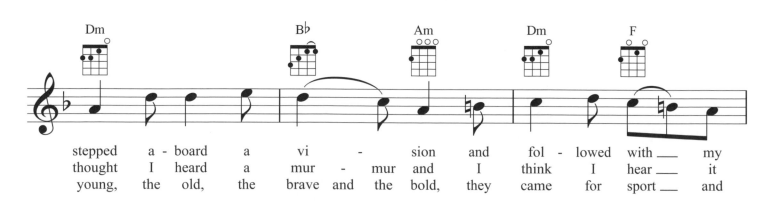

stepped a - board a vi - sion and fol - lowed with ___ my
thought I heard a mur - mur and I think I hear ___ it
young, the old, the brave and the bold, they came for sport ___ and

Additional Lyrics

4. I went to see my neighbors, to hear what they might say,
   The old ones were all dead and gone, the others turning grey.
   I met with tailor Quigley, he's as bold as ever still,
   Sure he used to make my britches when I lived in Spancil Hill.

5. I paid a flying visit to my first and only love,
   She's white as any lily and gentle as a dove.
   She threw her arms around me, saying, "Johnny, I love you still."
   She's Mag, the farmer's daughter and the pride of Spancil Hill.

6. I dreamt I stooped and kissed her as in the days of yore.
   She said, "Johnny, you're only joking, as many's the time before."
   The cock crew in the morning, he crew both loud and shrill,
   And I woke in California, many miles from Spancil Hill.

'Tis the Last Rose of Summer

Words by Thomas Moore
Music by Richard Alfred Milliken

The Wearing of the Green

Eighteenth Century Irish Folk Song

First note

Spirited

Verse

1. Oh ___ Pad - dy, dear, and did you hear the
(2.) since the col - or we must wear is
(3.) if at last our col - or should be

news that's go - ing 'round? The sham - rock is for - bid by law to
Eng - land's cru - el red, sure Ire - land's sons will ne'er for - get the
torn from Ire - land's heart, her sons, with shame and sor - row, from the

grow on I - rish ground. Saint ___ Pat - rick's Day no more to keep. His
blood that they have shed. You may take the sham - rock from your hat and
dear old soil will part. I've heard whis - pers of a coun - try that lies

col - or can't be seen, for there's a blood - y law a - gin' the
cast it on the sod, but 'twill take root and flour - ish still, though
far be - yond the sea, where rich and poor stand e - qual in the

Whiskey in the Jar

Traditional Irish Folk Song

First note

Verse
Moderately fast

1. As I was go - in' o - ver the Cork and Ker - ry
(2.) count - ed out his mon - ey; paid a pret - ty
(3.) ear - ly in the morn - ing, be - fore I rose to
(4.) *See additional lyrics*

moun - tains, met with Cap - tain Far - rell and his mon - ey he was
pen - ny. Put it in me pock - et and I took it home to
trav - el. Up rides a band of foot - men and like - wise __ rash - er

count - in'. I first pro - duced me pis - tol,
Jen - ny. And she sighed and she swore, _____
Far - rell. Well, I drew up - on me pis - tol,

then pro - duced __ me ra - pier. Sing, "Stand and de - liv - er. I
she nev - er would de - ceive me. The dev - il take the wom - en for they
she stole a - way me ra - pier. Could - n't shoot the wa - ter, so a

Additional Lyrics

4. Some take delight in the fishin' and the fowlin'.
   Others take delight in the carriage gently rollin'.
   Ah, but I take delight in the juice of the barley;
   Courtin' pretty women in the mountains of Killarney.
   Musha ring dumma doo-rama da.

Wild Rover

Traditional Irish Folk Song

First note

Verse
Moderately, with a lilt

1. I've been a wild rov - er for man - y a
(2.) in - to an ale - house I used to fre -
(3.) out of my pock - et I took sov - 'reigns
(4.) back to my par - ents, con - fess what I've

year, and I've spent all my mon - ey on
quent, and I told the land - la - dy my
bright, and the land - la - dy's eyes o - pened
done, and ask them to par - don their

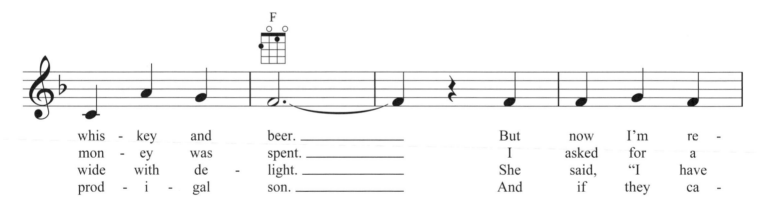

whis - key and beer. But now I'm re -
mon - ey was spent. I asked for a
wide with de - light. She said, "I have
prod - i - gal son. And if they ca -

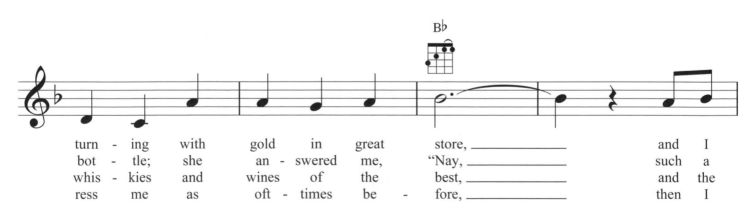

turn - ing with gold in great store, and I
bot - tle; she an - swered me, "Nay, such a
whis - kies and wines of the best, and the
ress me as oft - times be - fore, then I

nev - er will play the wild rov - er no more.
cus - tom as yours I can get an - y day."
words that I said, sure, were on - ly in jest."
nev - er will play the wild rov - er no more. } And it's

Chorus

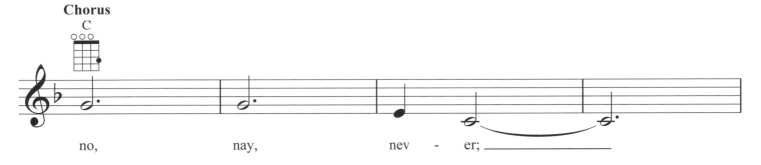

no, nay, nev - er; _____

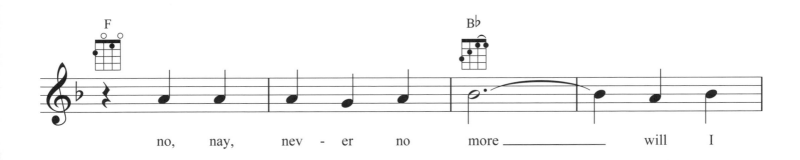

no, nay, nev - er no more _____ will I

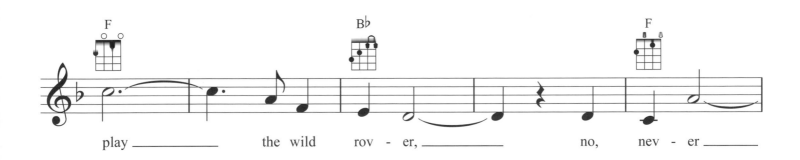

play _____ the wild rov - er, _____ no, nev - er _____

|1.–3.| |4.|

____ no more. _____ 2. I went more. _____
3. Then __
4. I'll go

When Irish Eyes Are Smiling

Words by Chauncey Olcott and George Graff, Jr.
Music by Ernest R. Ball

laugh - ter's like some fair - y song, and your eyes twin - kle
life is the sweet - est of all, there is ne'er a real

C7   F   D7

bright as can be, _____ you should laugh all the
care or re - gret. _____ And while spring - time is

G   D7

while and all oth - er times, while, and now smile ___ a
ours through - out all of youth's hours, let us smile ___ each

G   G7   **Chorus** C

smile for me. _____ } When I - rish
chance we get. _____ }

G7   C   C7   F

eyes are smil - ing, _____ sure it's like a

C   F

morn in spring. _____ In the lilt of

I - rish laugh - ter, you can hear the

an - gels sing. _____ When I - rish hearts are

hap - py, _____ all the world seems bright and

gay. _____ And when I - rish eyes are

smil - ing, sure they steal _____ your heart a -

1.
way. _____ 2. For your way. _____